Play Football!

Play Football!

by Tim Polzer

LONDON, NEW YORK, MUNICH,
MELBOURNE, AND DELHI

PROJECT EDITOR Elizabeth Hester
ART EDITOR Megan Clayton

PUBLISHER Chuck Lang
CREATIVE DIRECTOR Tina Vaughan
MANAGING EDITOR Beth Sutinis
PRODUCTION MANAGER Chris Avgherinos

Produced in partnership and licensed by
NFL Properties LLC

Cover designed by Bill Madrid

First American Edition, 2002
04 05 10 9 8 7 6 5 4

Published in the United States by
DK Publishing, Inc.
375 Hudson Street
New York, New York 10014

DK Publishing, Inc. offers special discounts for bulk purchases
for sales promotions or premiums. Specific, large-quantity
needs can be met with special editions, including personalized
covers, excerpts of existing guides, and corporate imprints.
For more information, contact
Special Markets Department, DK Publishing, Inc.,
375 Hudson Street, New York, New York 10014

Library of Congress Cataloging-in-Publication Data

Play football!.– 1st American ed.
   p. cm.
 ISBN 0-7894-8843-4
 1. Football–Juvenile literature. I. DK Publishing, Inc.
 GV950.7 .P53 2002
 796.332–dc21
                                         2002024497

Reproduced by Hong Kong Scanner, Hong Kong, China
Printed and bound in Spain by Artes Graficas Toledo.

Discover more at
www.dk.com

Contents

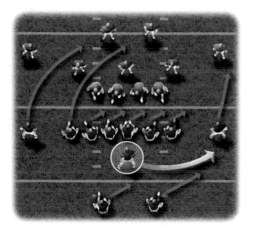

Introduction

A S A PARENT OF A YOUTH football player, you can get involved by supporting and encouraging your child. Help your children find and sign up for a league. Shop with them for equipment, and make sure they have the required uniform and safety gear. Show your interest by attending practice often and arriving at games on time.

Coaches must learn and adhere to league rules, and schedule and plan practices that are both effective and convenient for their players. Coaches not only give instruction and teach plays during practice, they should also be prepared to provide water and first aid during practices and games.

Football is a sport that teaches lessons in teamwork, concentration, preparation, and responsibility while kids are having fun and getting exercise. Keep in mind the following coaching principles to make sure everyone on your team has a positive experience:

MAKE IT FUN

Regardless of whether it's a game or a practice, football at the youth level should always be fun. This requires a little creativity on the coach's part, but with some thought and planning you can offer enjoyable practice activities and adopt kid-friendly methods throughout all aspects of your program. Incorporate games and low-key competitions to teach fundamentals rather than only running traditional drills.

LIMIT STANDING AROUND

Kids who find themselves waiting around in practice will eventually lose interest in the game. In both games and practices, engage every participant consistently. Offer young players an opportunity to have fun and their overall skills will improve. Attention and energy levels will improve when you involve every player in drills of short duration.

EVERYONE PLAYS

Football at the youth level should be an inclusive experience. It's never fun to sit and watch others participate, anticipating the opportunity to play only if the situation arises. The youth level of

football should be an equal learning experience for everyone, whether in a game or a practice.

TEACH EVERY POSITION TO EVERY PLAYER

A coach is a teacher. The coach's job is to raise the level of learning and skills of all players on his team, not just the most talented. Don't pigeonhole kids in one particular position because of their physical size and/or ability. A youth coach's job is to introduce and teach every position to every child on his or her team, so that each child will naturally find the position that's best for him or her.

EMPHASIZE THE FUNDAMENTALS

Build an uncrackable foundation by properly teaching the basics. Learning the fundamentals and perfecting the same basics at every level of play is essential to a player's and a team's success.

INCORPORATE A PROGRESSION OF SKILL DEVELOPMENT

For every participant, regardless of a player's skill level, it is the responsibility of a youth football coach to teach and encourage skill development. When kids experience improvement in their skills, no matter what their athletic ability may be, they will continue to participate and return to learn more.

YELL ENCOURAGEMENT, WHISPER CONSTRUCTIVE CRITICISM

Keep it positive. Youth football coaches and parents should never direct negative comments toward players or tolerate negative comments from players. Kids know when they've made mistakes and do not need to have that mistake compounded by negative feedback. Offer feedback that corrects a mistake while encouraging the player.

Play football!

FOOTBALL IS PLAYED WITH 11 players from each team on the field. Each team's objective is to pass, kick, or run the ball forward into the end zone, the 10-yard area at the end of the field where teams can score. Players also have to defend the end zone behind them, which is the other team's goal. Each player on the football field has a special—and very different—function in each play. Some are fast runners who carry the ball nimbly down the field, and some are tough tacklers who keep the other team from scoring. As you learn more about football, you'll figure out which position is right for you.

The field

The first football fields were really just fields. As the game grew in popularity and became more organized, the playing field was standardized. Field markings including yard-line numbers, hashmarks, and yardage stripes help players and officials on the field and spectators watching in the stands measure the progress of the ball and various players. A football field is sometimes called a gridiron because its lines were once marked off in a grid pattern.

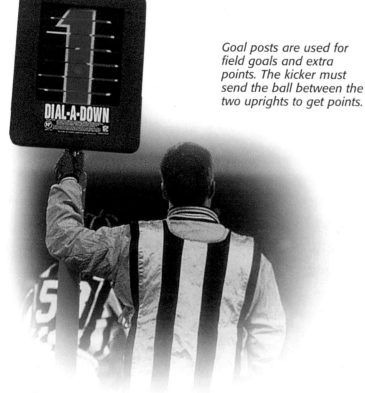

The field is a total of 120 yards long—100 yards of playing area and two 10-yard end zones.

Goal posts are used for field goals and extra points. The kicker must send the ball between the two uprights to get points.

DIAL-A-DOWN

Yard lines cross the field every five yards.

The goal line separates the end zone from the field of play. It must be crossed to score a touchdown.

First down

A play from scrimmage in football is called a down. When a team has the ball, it gets four downs to move the ball at least 10 yards. If the offense can do this by the end of the fourth down, the referee calls "first down," and the offense starts a new set of four downs with the ball in its new position. If not, the ball is turned over to the other team. Changeable down markers help players and fans keep track of play.

Who's on the field?

A football team has both offensive and defensive players on the roster, but only one group from each team is on the field at a time. In this diagram, the red team is playing offense, which means it has possession of the ball. The blue team is playing defense, trying to stop the ball from advancing. (The roles reverse when the blue team gains possession.) Look for this diagram throughout the book to highlight the players and formations connected with each skill.

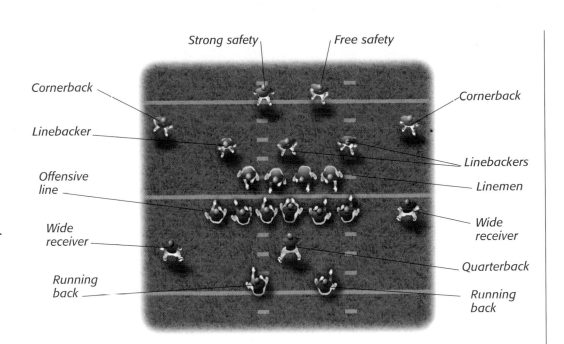

Strong safety
Free safety
Cornerback
Cornerback
Linebacker
Linebackers
Linemen
Offensive line
Wide receiver
Wide receiver
Quarterback
Running back
Running back

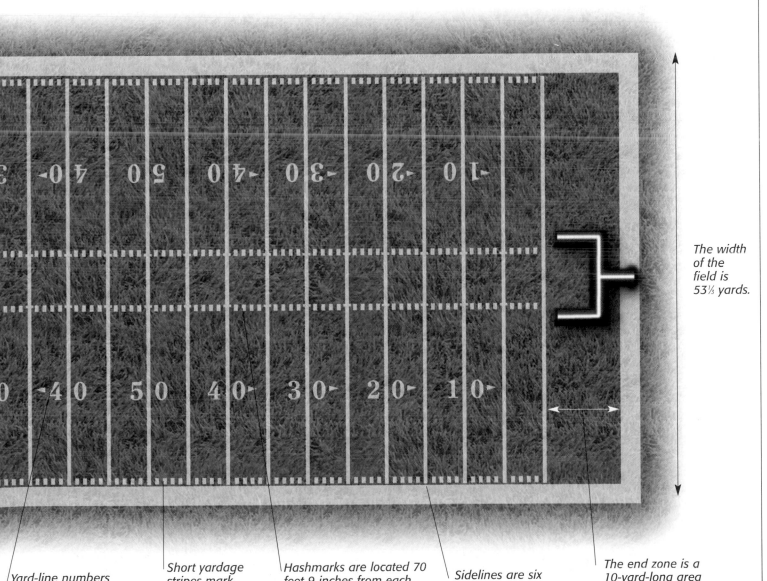

The width of the field is 53⅓ yards.

Yard-line numbers every 10 yards show the distance to the end zone.

Short yardage stripes mark each yard along the field.

Hashmarks are located 70 feet 9 inches from each sideline. The ball is placed between the two rows of hashmarks to start play.

Sidelines are six feet wide and mark the boundaries of the field.

The end zone is a 10-yard-long area at each end of the field. Touchdowns are scored here.

Who's who

IT'S IMPORTANT TO KNOW who's who in a football game—and what each person's job is. Everyone on the field or on the sidelines, from players to coaches to officials, has a specific function in the game. You can usually tell who does what by their uniforms.

Players

All members of a team wear uniforms of similar color so they contrast with the opposing team and make it easier to find each other on the field. Jerseys include numbers and sometimes names to distinguish between players on the same team. In the NFL, jersey numbers apply to specific positions. For example, numbers 80-89 are worn by wide receivers.

Coaches

Coaches are adults who teach you about football, help you improve your skills, and manage the team. In a game, coaches call plays and decide which players play when. Coaches are also there to answer your questions about football and help you if you are injured.

Referees

Game officials, or referees, wear black-and-white striped shirts. They are on the field during play, making sure the game goes smoothly.

Words to know

These football terms will be used throughout the book to describe plays, positions, and other parts of the game. Read over them now to get used to things you'll hear around the football field, or come back to this list later to look up new words.

Backfield The area behind the line of scrimmage.

Backpedal Backward running to drop into pass coverage.

Blitz A pass rush involving defensive backs or linebackers.

Block An offensive player moves a defensive player away from the ball.

Bootleg A play where the quarterback fakes a handoff and runs around the tight end.

Bump and run A pass defense in which the defender bumps the receiver at the line of scrimmage.

Center The middle offensive lineman that snaps the ball to the quarterback.

Cornerback One of two defensive backs positioned on the outside corners of the defense.

Defense The team without the ball. The defense tries to get the ball back and stop the offense from scoring.

Defensive backs The cornerbacks and safeties behind the linebackers.

Defensive ends The two players at the end of the defensive line.

Down A play from scrimmage. The offense gets four downs numbered in sequence, first to fourth, to gain 10 yards and make a new first down.

Eligible receiver Any of the five offensive players who are allowed to receive a pass.

End zone The area, 10 yards deep, bounded by the end line, goal line, and both sidelines. A team scores points by moving the ball into their opponent's end zone for a touchdown.

Extra point The one- or two-point play allowed a team after scoring a touchdown. Most youth teams go for two points.

Fair catch An unhindered catch by the receiver of a punt or kickoff. The returner raises one arm high over his head to signal a fair catch.

Forward pass A ball thrown, usually with an overarm motion, in the direction of the offense's goal line.

Four-point stance A stance with both hands on the ground, often used by defensive linemen.

Fumble Loss of possession of the football by the ball carrier or passer.

Goal line The field stripe separating the end zone and the field of play that must be crossed to score a touchdown.

Guards The two offensive linemen on either side of the center.

Half There are two halves to a game.

Halftime The intermission between the first and second halves of a game. Teams rest and discuss strategy during halftime.

Handoff A play in which the ball is given to another player, usually from a quarterback to a running back.

Hashmarks The short lines used to spot the ball on the field.

Holding The penalty called for illegal grabbing or use of hands.

Hole A space in the offensive line opened by blockers for a ball carrier to run through.

Huddle A brief gathering for play and signal calling by the offense and defense between plays.

I-formation A backfield formation featuring two running backs in line directly behind the quarterback.

Interception A change of possession when a defensive player catches a pass intended for an offensive player.

Lateral A toss or pass backward from the direction of play.

Linebacker A defender who plays between the defensive linemen and the defensive backs.

Line of scrimmage The imaginary line running from sideline to sideline on which the ball is snapped. It moves up and down the field with the ball.

Man-for-man A pass defense where each defender covers one receiver.

Nose tackle The defensive tackle in a 3-4 alignment who lines up opposite the center.

Offense The team that has the ball and is trying to score.

Pass rush A play in which defenders try to sack the passer.

Penalty A call made by the game official when a player breaks a rule. A penalty may result in a loss of yardage or a down.

Play-action pass A play in which the quarterback fakes a running play, then passes.

Pocket The area of protection around a passer formed by his blockers.

Possession When a team has the ball.

Punt A type of kick used primarily on fourth down.

Quarter There are four quarters in a game, two in each half.

Quarterback The player who leads the offense, calls plays, hands off the ball, runs with the ball, or passes it.

Rollout When the quarterback leaves the pocket, following blockers, to throw a pass.

Running backs The players who are the main ball carriers.

Sack When the quarterback is tackled in the backfield while attempting to pass.

Set When an offensive player gets into his stance.

Sidelines The lines running the length of the field, from end line to end line, marking the outside boundaries of the field and end zones. The sideline is out of bounds.

Snap When the center passes the ball to the quarterback to start a play.

Snap count The signal on which the ball is snapped.

Three-point stance A stance used by offensive and defensive linemen and running backs in which one hand is touching the ground.

Tight end A receiver/blocker position outside the offensive tackle.

Time out When a team or an official stops action and the clock.

Touchdown A six-point scoring play that occurs when one team crosses the other team's goal line with the ball in its possession.

Wide receiver A pass receiver who is set outside the offensive tackle.

Equipment

FOOTBALL EQUIPMENT IS DESIGNED to protect you from injury as much as possible while you play the game. Youth players use equipment that is similar to the gear worn by college and NFL players. It is important to learn how to wear your equipment properly. Always read the manufacturer's instructions and warnings that come with each piece.

Pads

Nobody sees the pads and guards that make up the first layer of your uniform, but in a game or practice, you'll be glad you have them. Pads protect you from run-ins with opponents and falls on the field by softening the impact on your body. There are lots of different kinds of padding, so be sure to learn which one goes where so you're properly protected.

Hand pads are worn by linemen and linebackers to protect their hands. Receivers, running backs, and defensive backs may wear gloves to improve their grip.

A helmet protects your head, ears, and face.

Stomach/hip pads are worn beneath the pants to provide protection and support for the hips and abdomen.

Some players wear neck rolls or collars to provide support for their necks.

Shoulder pads are worn beneath the jersey to cover your shoulders, upper arms, chest, and upper back.

Some players wear biceps pads to protect their upper arms.

Elbow pads help protect against hits from other players and scrapes from the field.

Forearm pads protect the lower arm.

Thigh pads are worn beneath the pants and protect the front of the thigh.

Knee pads are worn beneath the pants and protect the front of the knee.

Shin pads go underneath socks to protect the front of the lower leg.

Long cleats for natural grass

Tough, cleated shoes provide protection for your feet and traction on the field.

EXTRA POINT

On a cold and icy day at the Polo Grounds, the New York Giants trailed the Chicago Bears 13-3 at halftime of the 1934 NFL Championship Game. But the Giants changed to basketball shoes for better footing and roared to a 30-13 victory in what has come to be known as the Sneakers Game.

The ball

Footballs are made of a rubber bladder filled with air and covered with textured leather. Laces along the middle make it easier to grip and pass. High school, college, and youth league footballs often have white stripes around the ends. Youth footballs are also slightly smaller to fit young hands.

Laces for fingers to grip

Synthetic lining to protect air bladder

Hands

Many players wear gloves to protect their hands or help handle the ball. Taping your fingers and wrists can also help improve your grip and protect you from injury. If you tape or wrap your hands, be sure your wrists and fingers feel comfortable and have a full range of movement.

Some players tape their fingers to improve their grip. Never tape your fingers tight enough to cause pain or cut off blood flow.

Elastic wraps can protect your hands and provide support for injuries.

Shoes

The right shoes are important to keep you fast—and safe—on your feet. There are different choices for different games: long cleats for traction on grass, or short rubber cleats and flat soles to grip artificial turf. Either way, make sure your shoes fit comfortably and support your ankles.

Thick padding for a snug fit around the ankle

Holes for ventilation

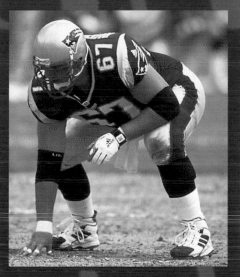

ON FIELD WITH THE PROS

This field has sections of dirt as well as grass, but New England Patriots offensive lineman Grey Ruegamer's high-top cleats provide good traction and ankle support for both. Good padding will also help ensure he's safe throughout the game.

Wrapping your ankle

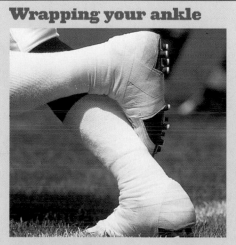

Properly wrapping your ankle with tape can help prevent ankle injury. Some NFL players also wrap their shoes. Always have a parent or coach wrap your ankles or feet.

Headgear

Headgear is one of the most important parts of equipment. It protects your head, ears, and face from injury. Always wear your helmet with chinstrap buckled and mouthpiece in.

The fit should not be too tight, but it should sit straight and not wobble.

Helmets

The helmet is made of rigid plastic to shield your head from hits during play. Inflatable pads inside the helmet provide extra cushioning and ensure a good fit. When your helmet fits correctly, you should have a clear view under the brow and be able to hear play calls through the ear holes.

A helmet should fit comfortably around your ears.

EXTRA POINT

The first NFL players wore leather helmets without facemasks.

The facemask should be high enough to protect your mouth and jaws.

The horseshoe-shaped part of a mouthpiece fits in your mouth. Hold it between your teeth during play.

Facemasks

NFL players wear a variety of facemasks. The size of the facemask depends on the player's position. Linemen, tight ends, and linebackers often wear large facemasks that cover their entire face. Quarterbacks, running backs, receivers, and defensive backs usually wear smaller facemasks that allow a greater field of vision.

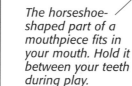

You should be able to see clearly from inside your helmet.

A mouthpiece is necessary to protect your mouth, teeth, and tongue. Always wear your mouthpiece on the field.

Mouthpiece

All youth players must wear mouthpieces during play. Mouthpieces help protect your teeth and tongue. Some mouthpieces attach to your helmet so they're easier to find when you need them. Ask your coach if it's okay to remove your mouthpiece between plays.

A plastic strap adjusts to fit your helmet. It bends to hold the mouthpiece in place.

A loop at the end of a mouthpiece connects it to the helmet so it won't get lost.

ON FIELD WITH THE PROS

Tight end Wesley Walls wears a full facemask to help protect his face while blocking and receiving. The strip on his nose is designed to help open his nasal passages and allow him to breathe easier.

Eye-black stickers

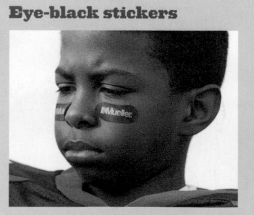

Eye-black stickers applied under the eyes help reduce glare from the sun. Before these stickers were invented, black grease was sometimes used.

Warming up

BEFORE YOU EXERCISE, your muscles are at rest, not ready for the strain or range of movement they'll need to play football. Taking time before each practice and game to warm up and stretch your body's muscles can help prepare you to play. Follow your coach's directions for warm-up. Proper warm-up and stretching increases your breathing rate, heart rate, and flexibility. Preparing your body this way can improve performance and reduce the chance of injury.

Warming up

Running laps at the beginning of practice is a good way to get your body moving and your muscles warmed up. You can also try running basic pass routes. Your coach can suggest specific passing drills and stretching exercises. Focus on stretching different muscle groups: calves, quads, groin, trunk, and shoulders.

Practice throwing

Passing with a teammate will help you loosen up your arm and get the feel of the ball at the beginning of practice. Take it easy—throw the ball lightly while your muscles are still warming up.

Stay hydrated

Because your body loses water when you perspire, it is important to drink plenty of water during time outs, breaks, and anytime you're off the field. Always take a bottle of water with you to practice and games.

Passing basics

A GOOD PASSER CAN HELP HIS team gain yardage quickly by passing to teammates downfield. With a throw to a receiver in the end zone, a passer can also help score touchdowns. Before making big plays on the field, though, it's important to warm up with the basics. Start with the correct grip and good passing form.

EXTRA POINT

Many NFL quarterbacks learned to play in youth football leagues. Some also participated in Punt, Pass & Kick competitions, which are open each fall to boys and girls ages 8–15.

Get a grip

A good pass begins with the correct grip. Using a youth-sized football, you should be able to hold the ball firmly. Keep your throwing hand at the back of the ball and your fingers over the laces. Cock your wrist before you throw the ball.

Two hands stay on the ball until you are ready to throw.

Keep your head up and your eyes on the target.

Grip the ball firmly, but not too tightly, as you bring it back.

Cock your wrist to throw.

Keep your elbow away from your body.

Passing drill

Concentrate on fundamentals when warming up for practice or a game. Try going through the basic motions of a throw to loosen up your arm and upper body. You can use the same steps to play catch—just add a release.

Aim as though you're throwing to a receiver.

Arm is extended up and away from the body

Snap your wrist.

1 Start by pulling the ball back with your arm fully extended. Cock your wrist to throw.

2 Keep your arm up when you practice your passes. Throw overhand for better accuracy.

3 Snap your wrist at the very end of the throw. (When practicing by yourself, you can hold onto the ball.)

John Elway

"Don't turn your head away as you throw. Snap your wrist as you release the ball for a good spiral."

Who passes?

The quarterback throws most of his team's passes, but running backs and receivers sometimes throw the ball, too.

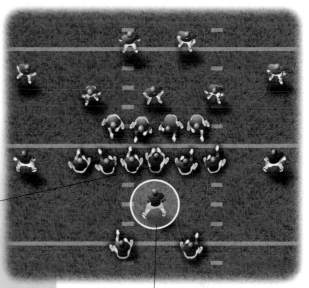

The center snaps the ball (tosses it to the quarterback) to start the play.

Keep your head up even at the end of your throw.

The quarterback stands behind the center of the offensive line. On a passing play, he takes the snap, drops back, and passes to a receiver.

Bring your arm across your body to follow through.

4 Practice following through, moving your arm and shoulder across your body.

ON FIELD WITH THE PROS

Peyton Manning keeps both hands on the ball while he looks for a receiver.

17

Throwing deep

I T TAKES MORE THAN A STRONG arm to be a good passer. Getting the ball safely into the hands of a receiver downfield requires accuracy, careful footwork, and timing. Practice will help you develop your own style, but a successful throw always starts with the basics: drop, takeback, release.

Drop, takeback, and release

When the ball is snapped, the quarterback retreats several steps from the line of scrimmage (the drop) to avoid the pass rush. When he locates a receiver, he cocks his arm (the takeback), and follows through (the release) as he throws a pass.

Keep your eyes on the receiver.

Nonthrowing hand points the receiver.

The ball is at head level.

Stay balanced, weight on both legs.

1 Look for receivers as you step back into your drop. Take the ball back outside your passing shoulder. Stop your drop. You should be evenly balanced on both feet, with the ball head high and your shoulder square to the receiver.

2 Point your nonthrowing hand toward the receiver, and step toward the receiver as you begin your pass.

The targets

Passers can throw only to eligible receivers: wide receivers (WR), tight ends (TE), and running backs (RB). When the ball is snapped on a passing play, these players run down the field or toward the sideline to find an open space that the quarterback can throw to.

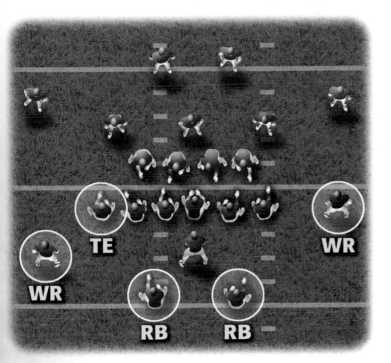

EXTRA POINT

Five other quarterbacks were selected ahead of Dan Marino in the 1983 NFL Draft, but he finished his 17-year career at the head of the class—setting career records for completions (4,967), passing yards (61,361), and touchdown passes (420).

Keep your body balanced.

3 Shift your weight from back to front as you bring the ball through your body. Try not to overthrow or lose your balance.

Keep your eyes on the receiver.

4 Create a spiral by snapping your wrist as you release the ball. Your weight should slightly shift to your front foot upon release.

Follow through across your body.

5 Keep your eyes on the receiver and always follow through, moving your arm and shoulder across your body toward the target.

Playing quarterback

THE QUARTERBACK IS THE LEADER of the offense. He calls the play in the huddle and then starts each play by taking the ball from the center. The quarterback is also called the passer because of his most important skill, but he needs good footwork and ball-handling skills, too.

Keep your shoulders square to the center. Do not look down at your hands.

Place your wrists together with your passing hand on top.

Pass pocket

The quarterback is protected by the offensive line, which forms a pocket to give him time to pass. The linemen can only hold off the defense for so long, though, so the passer has to act fast.

Receiving the snap

Every play from the line of scrimmage begins with a snap from the center to the quarterback. The quarterback stands behind the center with his hands ready to receive the ball.

Play-action pass

In this play, the quarterback fakes a handoff to confuse the defense. The quarterback then has time to find a receiver.

Running back runs at full speed.

Quarterback turns as if he will hand off.

Quarterback hides the ball.

Running back keeps his course.

Watch the running back.

Running back pretends to grab the ball.

1 Take the snap, hold the ball against your stomach, and pivot toward the running back as you would to hand off.

2 Hide the ball against your body. Reach your empty hand toward the running back.

3 Put your empty hand into the running back's stomach. Pull it out as he runs past.

ON FIELD WITH THE PROS

When no receivers are open for a pass, quarterback Rich Gannon runs with the ball himself. After passing the line of scrimmage, though, a quarterback cannot pass the ball forward.

Quarterbacks must be able to see over and around the blockers to look for receivers.

The tight end can block or run out for a pass, depending on which play is called.

Running back runs as if he has the ball.

Quarterback turns around.

Quarterback begins proper passing form.

Running back can block or run out for a pass.

4 Hide the ball close to your body. Drop back away from the running back.

5 Stop your drop and find an open receiver. Bring back your arm and prepare to throw.

Three- and seven-step drops

Quarterbacks usually drop back three steps for short pass plays and seven steps for longer pass plays.

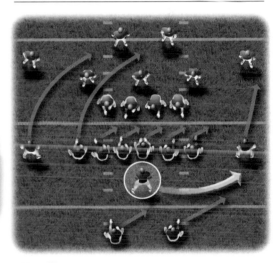

Rollout

The quarterback takes the snap and then carries the ball left or right with the rest of the offense.

Bootleg

The quarterback takes the snap and then fakes a handoff and switches direction.

Ready to run

RUNNING WITH THE BALL, or rushing, is another way an offense can gain yardage. Rushers (usually running backs) must get the ball from the quarterback in a handoff, run whichever play is called, and protect the ball from the defense. They've got to be fast—and sometimes have a couple of tricks up their sleeves—to move the ball into scoring position.

Explosive stance

Running backs usually begin each play in a three-point stance. From this stance, it's easier to take off with speed and energy toward the line of scrimmage at the snap. Remember, running backs are allowed to run parallel to the line of scrimmage before the play starts, but once in your stance, no movement is permitted before the snap.

EXTRA POINT

Eric Dickerson holds the NFL record for most rushing yards gained in a season with 2,105 in 1984.

Keep your head up and still while you wait for the snap.

Watch the ball until it's snapped. The defense will be watching your eyes to guess your next move, so don't give anything away!

Your dominant arm goes in front.

Keep your weight centered over your hips.

Bend your knees. Do not squat.

Feet should be shoulder-width apart, dominant foot slightly behind the other foot.

Place your fingers on the ground for balance.

Taking a handoff

Rushers get the ball from the quarterback through a handoff. The quarterback waits while the running back approaches, then puts the ball in his hands so the rusher can run it down the field.

Keep your eyes on the hole. Do not look at the ball.

Make a good target for the ball to come to you—don't grab it.

The quarterback places the ball in your stomach.

1 Running backs should give the quarterback a large target in which to place the ball. You can do this by placing your arm nearest the quarterback near your chest and the other arm below your stomach.

2 As you approach the quarterback, keep your eyes on the hole through which you want to run. Do not look at the ball. Close your arms around the ball when you feel it hit your stomach.

Running backs

Running backs carry the ball on most rushing plays. They line up behind the quarterback, then move forward to take the handoff.

The offensive line creates a hole for the running back to run through.

Quarterbacks sometimes rush the ball, too.

Running backs can run in motion parallel to the line of scrimmage before they put their hands down into stance.

ON FIELD WITH THE PROS

Running back Fred Taylor demonstrates the proper form for taking a handoff (from quarterback Mark Brunell).

Handling the ball

AFTER TAKING THE HANDOFF, a running back must carry the ball forward to gain yards. Defenders try to tackle the ball carrier or cause her to fumble, or drop the ball. Proper handling technique and teamwork help keep the ball safe from the defense and give you a chance of scoring.

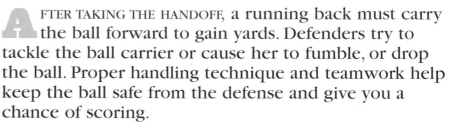

Keep your head up and look out for defenders.

Square your shoulders to run between the linemen.

Carry the ball with two hands to make it harder for defenders to knock it out.

Hold the ball in front of you, close to your stomach.

Protecting the ball

Hold the ball as if the other team is going to try to knock it out of your hands.

Run with the ball cradled between your body and the crook of your arm.

Watch where you are running. Do not look down at the ball as you shift your arms.

Shift the ball to the arm nearest the sideline. If you fumble, the ball should go out of bounds.

1 Carry the ball with two hands while you run through the hole, or when defenders are near.

2 When you've run past the defenders, switch the ball to one arm to help you run faster.

PRO TIP **Eddie George**

"Cover the ball up at all times. Protect it with your heart and put two hands on the ball so defenders can't knock it out."

I-formation

This type of formation allows the first running back (the fullback) to carry the ball or block for the second running back (the tailback).

The fullback can take the handoff or block for the tailback.

The tailback can run forward or around the tight end.

ON FIELD WITH THE PROS

Emmitt Smith is ready to put both hands on the ball if a defender nears.

Follow the fullback

In this handoff play, the tailback takes the ball and follows the fullback's blocking through the hole.

Tailback follows the lead.

Fullback leads the play.

1 Both running backs run toward the hole at the snap.

2 Keep your eyes on the hole, not the quarterback.

Get ready to take the ball.

Fullback goes after the defender.

3 The tailback opens his arms and looks for the fullback. The quarterback hands off the ball.

Try not to run into the fullback—let him lead the way.

Fullback protects the ball carrier.

4 Once you've got the ball, head for the hole. Run left or right of the fullback's block.

Running game

I**N RUNNING PLAYS, A RUNNING BACK** rushes, or runs with the ball, to gain yards for the offense. Rushers have to work with their teammates to get through the defense.

Finding the hole

Running backs take the handoff from the quarterback, then run between offensive linemen with the ball. It's the linemen's job to create a path through the defense.

The quarterback takes the snap and pivots left or right before handing the ball to the running back.

7 5 3 1 2 4 6

1

3 2

Running plays

The quarterback calls each running play as a two-digit code. The first number (orange) identifies a ball carrier. The second number (yellow) refers to the offensive line hole to run through.

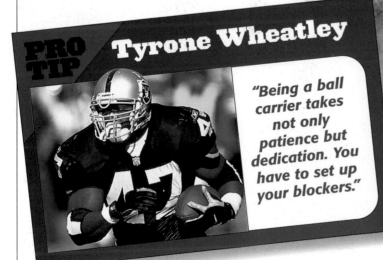

PRO TIP — **Tyrone Wheatley**

"Being a ball carrier takes not only patience but dedication. You have to set up your blockers."

ON FIELD WITH THE PROS

Ahman Green accelerates through the hole created by his linemen. Running backs must run quickly to get through the hole and gain yards.

A successful running play requires good timing between the quarterback and the running back beginning at the snap.

On most rushing plays, the running route is between two blockers.

Some plays call for the running back to run outside the tight end.

Offensive linemen will try to push defenders away from the hole.

On the line

Offensive linemen work together to push defenders away from the running holes and protect the ball carrier. They hold off the defense as long as they can, but the quarterback and running back must act quickly to move the ball.

Running backs must remember their position numbers and the offensive hole numbers.

Catch the ball

CATCHING A PASS FROM THE quarterback is one way to gain yards for your offense. It takes good hand-eye coordination and a lot of concentration to catch a pass like a pro. Play catch with a teammate or family member to practice your technique.

Making the catch

After the passer throws the ball in the air, receivers must judge where the ball is going and adjust their hands, arms, and body to make the catch.

Hands are close together, fingers spread.

Stay focused on the ball.

Keep your hands and fingers open.

Upper body is turned toward the ball.

Knees are bent so you're ready to go in any direction.

1 Follow the flight of the ball with your hands. Be sure to watch the speed and angle of the ball as it approaches.

2 Keep your eyes on the ball. Be sure to keep them open as the ball nears. Relax your hands and fingers.

PRO TIP — **Tim Brown**

"If the ball is above your head, put your thumbs together. If the ball is below your chest, put your pinky fingers together."

Let the ball stop spinning in your hands before you bring it into your body.

3 Allow your hands to give with the ball as your fingers close. Steady the ball, then bring it into your body.

By standing with one foot slightly behind the other, NFL receivers such as Randy Moss are ready to run when the ball is snapped.

A receiver can't move until the play begins, so Isaac Bruce takes a look down the line of scrimmage to watch for the snap.

Catching on the run

In a game situation, you'll usually be on the move during a play. Once you've got catching basics mastered, practice catching while you run.

EXTRA POINT

Legendary receiver Raymond Berry honed his skills in practice by asking to be thrown inaccurate passes.

1 Turn your head and shoulders toward the passer.

2 Find the ball and bring your hands up.

3 Adjust your speed to the flight of the ball.

4 Watch the ball all the way into your hands.

Receiving

RECEIVERS STAR IN SOME of the most glamorous plays in a game. A successful long pass can gain a lot of yards in a hurry—and maybe even result in a touchdown. Receivers have to concentrate on the ball, know how to catch from any position, and learn receiving routes that help the quarterback know where to throw the pass.

Begin bringing your hands together as the ball approaches.

Your eyes should follow the ball, not your hands.

PRO TIP

James McKnight

"Watch the point of the ball as it comes to you, but grab the fat of the ball."

Over-the-shoulder catch

You make this type of catch when the quarterback throws the ball from behind you.

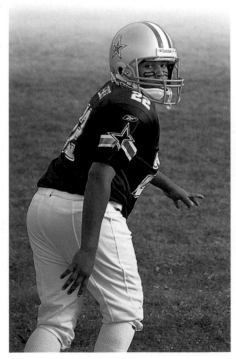

1 Turn your head and shoulders toward the passer as you run.

2 Move your arms and hands into position to catch the ball.

3 Twist your upper body with the ball as it approaches.

Sideline catch

Receivers must keep their feet in bounds when making a catch near the sideline. Know where the sideline is as you run your route. Plant your feet inside the sideline just before the ball arrives, and don't move your feet out of bounds until after the catch.

Watch the ball all the way into your hands.

The hand nearest the sideline goes under the ball.

Plant both feet inside the sideline.

EXTRA POINT

Jerry Rice has gained more than 20,000 yards receiving and caught a pass in more than 200 consecutive games.

4 Your head and eyes should follow the ball all the way into your hands.

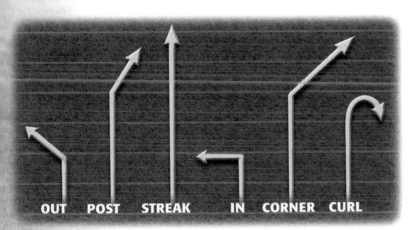

OUT   POST   STREAK   IN   CORNER   CURL

Receiving routes

Many coaches use the above terms for basic receiving routes. These routes tell the receiver where to run and the quarterback where to throw.

ON FIELD WITH THE PROS

Wide receiver Joe Horn demonstrates classic receiving form—hands apart, fingers spread wide, and eyes on the ball—as he twists to make an over-the-shoulder catch.

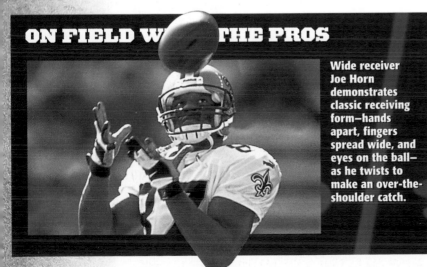

Running after the catch

With the ball securely in your hands, turn your head and look upfield.

After you make the catch, move the ball into the crook of your arm.

You can gain more yards by running with the ball after the catch. Always watch the ball all the way into your hands—you might drop the pass if you try to run before the catch.

Offensive line

OFFENSIVE LINEMEN PUSH, OR BLOCK, DEFENDERS to help other offensive players move the ball. They protect the quarterback so he has as much time as possible to get the ball to a teammate, and try to make room for the ball carriers to run.

Lineman's stances

Offensive linemen use a four-point stance (left) or a three-point stance (right). After putting a hand down, or getting set, a lineman cannot move until the ball is snapped. Keep your weight balanced and your eyes on the player in front of you while you listen for the snap count. Don't watch the ball!

Keep your head up and your eyes on the player in front of you.

Keep your weight balanced over your knees.

Anchor your feet for good traction.

ON FIELD WITH THE PROS

Patriots lineman Mike Compton shows the proper three-point stance. This stance allows him to keep his head up to see the defender and step forward or back the instant the ball is snapped without losing his balance.

Do not line up with your feet touching.

Leave some space between you and your teammate.

Offensive line split

Offensive linemen should start each play with an equal distance between each other. Be careful that your feet don't touch or overlap with another player to avoid trips and falls.

Heads and hands must stay behind the ball at the line of scrimmage.

Keep your back straight.

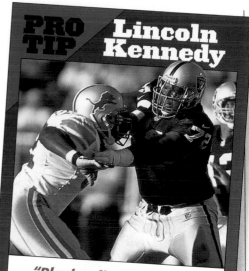
You can rest your other hand on your knee, but don't lean on it.

Use your hand for balance—but don't put too much weight on it.

The quarterback yells the snap count.

Keep your shoulders up and your back straight.

Keep your weight balanced over your knees—not the ball.

Place one hand on the ball. (If you need to, use two.)

Offensive line players include the center (C), left guard (LG), left tackle (LT), right guard (RG), right tackle (RT), and tight end (TE). They start each play along the line of scrimmage, then try to block the defense.

TE LT LG C RG RT

Center snap

The center starts the play at the middle of the offensive line, leaning over the ball. He puts a hand on the ball, waits for the snap count (the signal for the ball to be hiked, or snapped), and swings the ball between his legs, into the quarterback's hands. After the snap, the center blocks with the offensive line.

Blocking

BLOCKING IS AN IMPORTANT PART of offense. Without blockers to hold off defenders, passers could not pass and ball carriers could not run to gain yards. Linemen use different blocking techniques for passing plays and running plays.

Pass blocking

Offensive linemen must stay on their feet and be ready to stop pass rushers—defenders trying to sack or pressure the quarterback.

Keep both hands open.

1 Take a step forward and put your open hands on the defender.

Hands stay on the chest—don't touch the helmet or facemask.

2 Keep your hands high and push the defender.

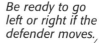

Be ready to go left or right if the defender moves.

3 Keep your feet moving and stay balanced.

Run blocking

Begin in a three-point stance. This allows you to step quickly and strongly into the defender.

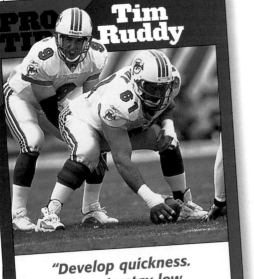

PRO TIP — Tim Ruddy

"Develop quickness. Learn to stay low coming off the ball."

Keep your back straight.

1 Line up with your teammates and take your stance. Keep your head up and listen for the snap count.

Stay low. Bend at the waist and knees.

2 When the quarterback calls the snap, step toward the defender you are supposed to block. Stay low, but keep your head up.

Stick to your defender until the end of the play.

Lean in and use your weight to stop the defender.

4 Keep blocking until the whistle blows.

ON FIELD WITH THE PROS

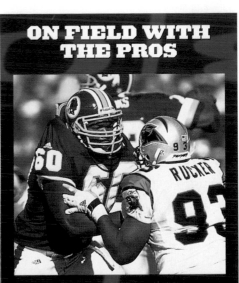

Chris Samuels blocks a pass rusher to protect the quarterback.

Willie Anderson positions himself between a defender and the ball carrier.

Hands stay open as you push the defender. Don't grab.

Keep your feet and legs moving before and after contact.

3 Raise your arms as you prepare to make contact with the defender. Keep your elbows bent, ready to push forward.

Protecting the quarterback

While the quarterback is in the pass pocket, he's protected by the offensive line. Linemen block defenders to give the passer time to find a receiver and throw the ball. They stay close together, forming a pocket around the quarterback to stop defenders from making a sack.

Defensive line

THE DEFENSIVE LINE GOES head to head with the offense at the line of scrimmage. Defensive linemen must push through blockers to tackle running backs. On passing plays, they try to sack the quarterback.

Power stance

A proper stance at the line of scrimmage allows defensive linemen to be quick and strong off the snap.

Before the snap

Defenders must wait for the ball or the offensive linemen to move. Before the snap, defensive linemen should watch the player in front of them and be ready to move when they do.

Keep your head and shoulders up. Your eyes should be on the player in front of you.

Balance your weight over your knees. Your knees should be about shoulder-width apart.

Anchor your feet for traction.

Do not put too much weight on your hand.

DE DT DT DE

Who's on the line?

Defensive linemen include defensive tackles (DT) and defensive ends (DE). Some teams use a single player called the nose tackle or nose guard in place of the two defensive tackles.

EXTRA POINT

Michael Strahan set the NFL record for most sacks in a season with 22½ in 2001.

Pass rush spin

To get past a blocker trying to guard the quarterback, a pass rusher can push a blocker back or spin out of the block.

Use your arms to push the blocker's arms down and away from you.

1 Push the blocker's hands away from your body.

Turn your body away from the blocker.

2 Spin out of the block, away from the blocker's hold.

Turn your body away from the blocker.

3 Turn upfield and find the quarterback.

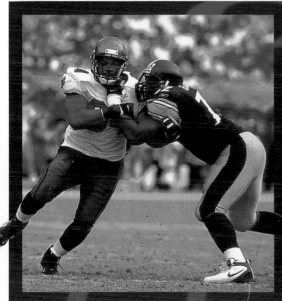

ON FIELD WITH THE PROS

Defensive tackle Warren Sapp (far left) uses his hands to keep a blocker away from his body. His strength and quickness make Sapp one of the NFL's best pass rushers.

Pass rushers do not always have to run through a blocker. Defensive end Chike Okeafor (far right) uses his speed and agility to run around the offensive lineman and sack the quarterback.

Linebackers

LINEBACKERS ARE RESPONSIBLE FOR helping stop both running plays and pass plays. They've got to be versatile enough to cover pass receivers, and tough enough to stop ball carriers.

Linebackers

Linebackers stand up behind the defensive line. During the play, they can be found all over the field— stopping a rusher, covering a receiver, or trying to sack the quarterback, or tackle him before he gives away the ball.

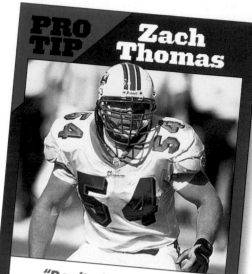

Linebackers are the middle defense— behind the linemen and in front of the defensive backs.

Blockers try to stop the linebackers from tackling the ball carrier.

Lateral pursuit

Linebackers are responsible for defending the area just behind the line of scrimmage. To stop rushers, linebackers shuffle from side to side so the ball carrier doesn't get through the hole. On pass plays, linebackers help stop the receivers.

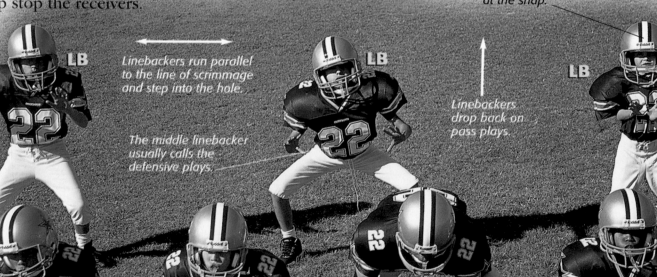

Linebackers watch the quarterback and running backs at the snap.

Linebackers run parallel to the line of scrimmage and step into the hole.

The middle linebacker usually calls the defensive plays.

Linebackers drop back on pass plays.

LB LB LB

Bracing for the play

A linebacker must be ready to react the moment the ball is put into play.

Keep your head up and your eyes on the quarterback at the snap.

Keep your hands up and ready to push blockers away.

Bend your knees and stay on your toes. Be prepared to run any direction.

Feet should be shoulder-width apart.

ON FIELD WITH THE PROS

Brian Urlacher is on his toes, ready to chase a running back or cover a receiver. In ready position, this stance lets him see over the defensive line to his targets on the offense.

EXTRA POINT

Linebacker Derrick Thomas set an NFL record in 1990 with 7 sacks in one game.

Defensive secondary

THE DEFENSIVE SECONDARY IS THE last line of defense. Defensive backs try to stop receivers from catching the ball and getting into scoring range. They can either knock the pass away or try to catch it themselves for an interception. Defensive backs can also help the linebackers make a tackle.

Pass coverage

Defensive backs cover receivers to keep them from catching passes. In a man-for-man defense, defensive backs usually play either basic or bump-and-run coverage.

Bump and run
The defensive back tries to slow the pass play by making contact with the receiver at the line of scrimmage.

Keep your eyes on the receiver, not the snap.

Put your arms in front of you, palms open.

Keep your knees bent and feet shoulder-width apart.

1 Line up in front of the receiver. Stay on your side of the line of scrimmage. Watch the receiver.

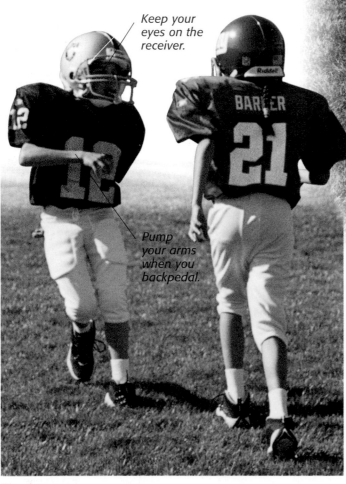

Keep your eyes on the receiver.

Pump your arms when you backpedal.

BARLER 21

Basic coverage
Stand a few yards from the line of scrimmage, across from the receiver. At the snap, backpedal. Keep the receiver in front of you so you can react and adjust to her direction and speed. If she runs around you, stop, turn, and run with her.

PRO TIP — **Eric Allen**

"When you're backpedaling, make sure you concentrate on the receiver rather than the quarterback."

The receiver may push you or try to run around you.

2 Use your hands to push and slow the receiver. If the receiver breaks free, follow down the field to cover the pass.

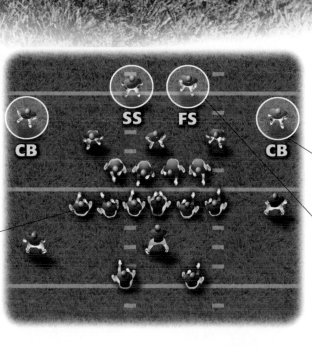
Defensive secondary

Defensive backs include cornerbacks (CB), strong safety (SS), and free safety (FS).

SS FS

CB CB

Cornerbacks try to keep ball carriers from running outside.

Safeties also help stop running plays.

Tight ends are covered by safeties on pass plays.

EXTRA POINT

Former Vikings safety Paul Krause owns the NFL record for career interceptions with 81.

Kicking

AT THE BEGINNING OF EACH HALF and after every score, play begins again with a kickoff. Kicking off is a way to turn the ball over to members of the other team when it's their turn to play offense. The kicker kicks the ball off a tee, and the receiving team catches it and tries to run the ball back to get close to its goal. Players on the kicking team run to stop the receivers' progress and keep them out of scoring range.

EXTRA POINT

NFL teams kick off from the 30-yard line. College and high school teams kick off from the 35-yard line.

Signal the referee with your hand.

Eyes on the ball

Lean back slightly as you kick.

The tee holds the ball until it is kicked.

Strike low on the ball to get more air and distance.

1 Raise your hand to signal that you are ready to kick off. Wait until the referee blows the whistle to start the game.

2 Run toward the ball slowly. Stay balanced and under control. Keep your head down and eyes on the ball.

3 As you arrive at the ball, plant your nonkicking foot and strike the lower half of the ball with your kicking foot.

Covering the kick

The kicker approaches the ball in the center of the field, between the rows of hashmarks. His teammates spread out to cover the width of the field. They have to stay behind the line where the ball is teed up until it is kicked. Then they follow the kick down the field to stop the receiving team from running it back.

Members of the kicking team line up across the field, ready to run after the ball and cover receivers.

Keep your balance as you follow through.

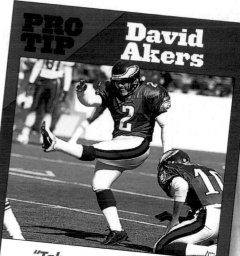

PRO TIP — **David Akers**

"Take a comfortable approach to the ball. Swing your foot powerfully."

Follow through with your leg.

4 Kick through the ball and follow through with your leg. Bring your arm around, letting your body turn with the follow-through.

The knee of your nonkicking leg should be slightly bent.

ON FIELD WITH THE PROS

You may see kickers such as Olindo Mare kick field goals and extra points in an NFL game. Most youth teams do not attempt these kicks because they are difficult for young players.

Punting

IF A FOOTBALL TEAM HAS not gained enough yards for a first down, it may choose to use its fourth down to punt. A punt turns the ball over to the defense, but leaves them farther from their goal than other kinds of turnovers. Unlike a kickoff, a punt begins with a snap from the center. But both types of kick have the same result: The receiving team tries to run the kick back as far as possible, and the kicking team tries to stop them.

Punting grip

Hold the ball with two hands to steady it after the snap and prepare for the drop. For this right-footed kicker, the right hand goes at the back of the ball. Left-footers do the opposite.

Punting sequence

Eyes on the ball

Hands are open, ready to catch.

1 Call your signal for the center to snap the ball. Use both hands to make the catch.

Watch the ball as it drops.

2 Take two steps. (The third step will be your kick.) Use your kicking-side hand to drop the ball just above your kicking foot. Keep your eyes on the ball.

Hold the ball in front of you.

Remove your second hand from the ball, leaving room for your leg to swing.

Step slowly toward the ball.

Center snaps the ball to the punter

The punter's place

The punter usually stands 10 to 15 yards behind the center. Players on the punting team—except for the center and two outside players—cannot run downfield until the punter kicks the ball.

Punter stands here

Deep snap

On punting plays, the center must make a long, or deep, snap to get the ball to the punter behind him.

1 Use two hands to hold the ball. Keep your weight over your knees.

2 Look through your legs to see the punter. Aim for his hands.

3 On the punter's signal, swing your arms hard to snap the ball.

Kicking foot is flat as it meets the ball

Nonkicking knee is slightly bent

3 Extend your kicking foot to meet the ball. Make your foot as flat as possible so the ball will go straight ahead.

Follow through with your leg.

Lean back slightly as your leg goes up

4 Kick the ball in the air. As you follow through, lean back slightly—but don't fall over!

Fair catch

If a punt returner chooses not to run the ball back, she can call "fair catch" by waving an arm while the ball is in the air. (It's a good idea to call fair catch if you think the other team will reach you before the ball does.) In exchange for making it illegal for the other team to hit her during the play, she gives up the right to run the ball after it's caught. The receiving team will get the ball where she catches it.

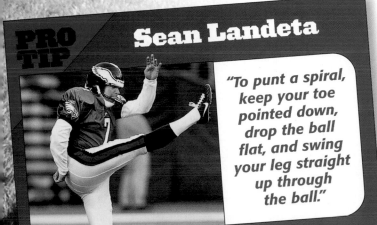

PRO TIP

Sean Landeta

"To punt a spiral, keep your toe pointed down, drop the ball flat, and swing your leg straight up through the ball."

Sportsmanship

EXTRA POINT

NFL rules allow players to throw, or spike, the ball to the ground after a score. College, high school, and most youth leagues do not allow spikes or other kinds of celebration or bragging on the field.

FOOTBALL IS A GREAT SPORT to enjoy as a team. But in order for everyone to have fun, it's important to practice good sportsmanship. Respect your teammates and your opponents. Listen to your coach and game officials. With a little bit of effort, the game can be a lot more fun for everyone. So play fair—and enjoy!

Respect your opponents

Win or lose, you and your teammates should shake hands with members of the other team after the game and congratulate them on playing well. Football is competitive, but you should show your opponents respect. Don't taunt or make fun of them if they make a mistake, or brag if your team does well.

Lend a hand

After a play, offer your teammates and opposing players a hand in getting off the ground.

46

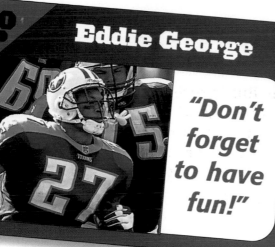

Follow the rules

Your coach should teach you the rules to play by. When a player breaks a rule, it's called a penalty, and can hurt your team. Referees and game officials are there to watch out for penalties and help you enjoy the game. Show officials respect. Do not argue their decisions or penalties. Let your coach ask the officials questions.

Applaud injured players

When an injured player leaves the field, cheer and yell encouragement. No one likes to be out of the game with an injury, so show that you wish him well.

Index

Photo credits

All instructional photos by Kevin Terrell and
Chris Choi of NFL Photos

Player photographs as listed below:

17 John Elway by James D. Smith
17 Peyton Manning by Allen Kee
19 Dan Marino by William Sallaz
21 Rich Gannon by Paul Jasienski
23 Mark Brunell, Fred Taylor
    by Greg Crisp
24 Eddie George by Marty Morrow
25 Emmitt Smith by Kevin Terrell/NFLP
26 Ahman Green by Todd Rosenberg
26 Tyrone Wheatley by Greg Crisp
28 Tim Brown by John Sandhaus
29 Randy Moss by Al Messerschmidt
29 Isaac Bruce by Kevin Terrell/NFLP

30 James McKnight by Al Pereira
31 Joe Horn by Joe Patronite
32 Mike Compton by Jennifer Abelson
33 Lincoln Kennedy by Greg Trott
34 Tim Ruddy by J.C. Ridley
35 Chris Samuels by Bill Wood
35 Willie Anderson by Joe Robbins
37 Warren Sapp by Al Messerschmidt
37 Chike Okeafor by Dave Stluka
37 Hugh Douglas by James D. Smith
38 Zach Thomas by Joe Robbins
39 Brian Urlacher by Joe Robbins
40 Eric Allen by Joe Sandhaus
41 Troy Vincent by Greg Crisp
43 David Akers by Greg Crisp
43 Olindo Mare by Steven Murphy
45 Sean Landeta by Jim Morton
47 Eddie George by Allen Kee

Acknowledgments

Thanks to all the National Football
League players who contributed their
instructional tips and advice for youth
football players.

Thanks to our youth players: Larissa
Campa, Sammy Carter, Paul Carter,
Christopher Cumming, Connor Garrity,
Hannah Hull, Daniel Pickens,
Alex Seibert, and Rebecca Wang

Special thanks to:
Sarita Borojevic, Culver City High School,
Culver City Unified School District, Henry
Gonzalez, Carol Lucas, Scott Macrillo,
Reebok, Riddell, South Gate Youth Football,
Wilson Sports, Lori Quenneville of the NFL